FOLENS

getting personal

1

CW01582750

Contents

Deena Haydon
Pat King
Christine Moorcroft

Myself and others

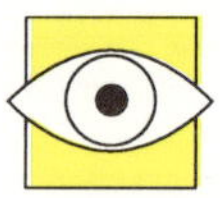

1. With a partner talk about all the things you notice about the children in the photograph.

2. Think of six of your own features. How many others in the class have the same features?

Feature	Me	Others
brown hair		
grey eyes		

Key Idea: How we are similar and different from others

3. Draw a person with short brown hair, blue eyes, long black eyelashes, brown eyebrows, a smiling mouth, a long straight nose and pierced ears.

4. Make a display of all the pictures made by your group. How are the pictures the same? How are they different?

People may have similar features but still look very different. They can be different in other ways.

5. Think of three things that make the person next to you special. Tell them. What do they think?

6. Make a badge or a certificate to show why you are special.

How could you show a friend that he or she is special?

Feelings

Changing feelings

Things around us can affect our feelings.

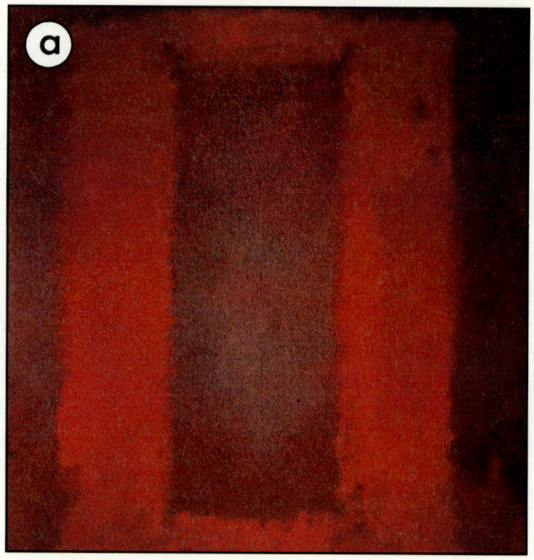

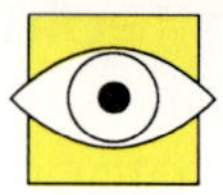

1. How do these paintings make you feel?

Write the words that describe how the picture makes you feel.

Painting	Feelings
a	
b	

Word bank

I feel ...

happy	like singing
joyful	like skipping
afraid	like crying
miserable	like dancing
sad	like running away

2. In a group, find out if others chose words like yours.

3. What is it about each picture that makes you feel the way you do?

Picture **a** makes me feel ______ because ________

Picture **b** makes me feel ______ because ____________ .

Key Idea: Feeling good, feeling bad

4. With a partner, think of four words that describe feeling good and four words that describe feeling bad.

Feeling good	**Feeling bad**

Make a display of everybody's words.

5. In pairs, take turns to talk about a time when you felt really good.

What made you feel like that?

6. Use a dictionary to find out what 'consequences' means.

7. What were the consequences of what Yasmin felt?

What could the children have done to change the consequences?

If you knew these children what advice would you give them?

What is a friend?

Good friends

1. How can you tell that these children are friends?

2. Talk in a group. What is special about a good friend? Share your ideas with the class.

3. Write an advertisement describing the kind of friend you would like.

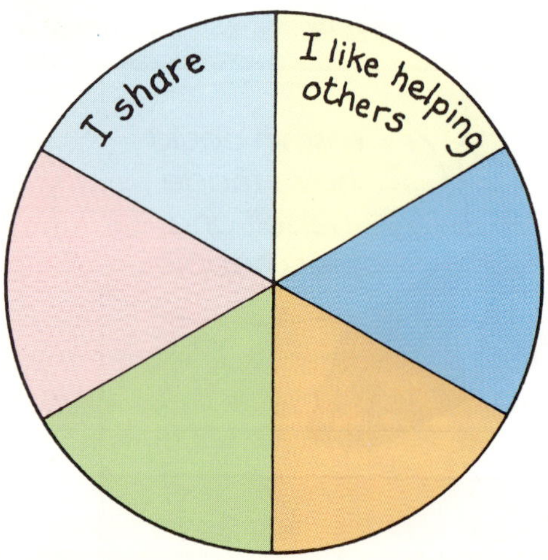

4. Would you be a good friend? Think of six qualities that make you a good friend. Copy and complete a friendship circle.

You may like doing some things together and some apart.

5. Draw two things that you like doing with a friend.

When did you last tell your friends that you like them?

6. Send a happigram to someone you care about. It might be a friend, someone you want to be friends with or a member of your family.

7. Some people find it hard to make friends. They may be shy or nervous. How could you help them?

How could you help someone who is new in your group?

Changing friends

1. Talk to others about how Sara might feel.

2. Describe her feelings now and in three months time. The word bank may help.

3. How might Zahid feel?

Word bank

afraid	excited
scared	sorry
upset	worried
happy	settled
sad	miserable
pleased	hopeful

4. Imagine your friend moved away.

Write a note telling your friend how you feel.
How might your friend feel in a few weeks?

Some friends live far away and never meet.
We call them pen-friends.
They write to each other.

5. Write a letter introducing yourself to a new pen-friend.

How is this different from a letter to an old friend?

There are other reasons for friends being separated.
Talk about them in your group.

How could you keep in touch with your friends?

Rules

Fair play

Citizenship

1. Why did the children want to play without rules?

2. Did they enjoy the game? Why was this?

3. Make up a board game or card game. Write the rules.

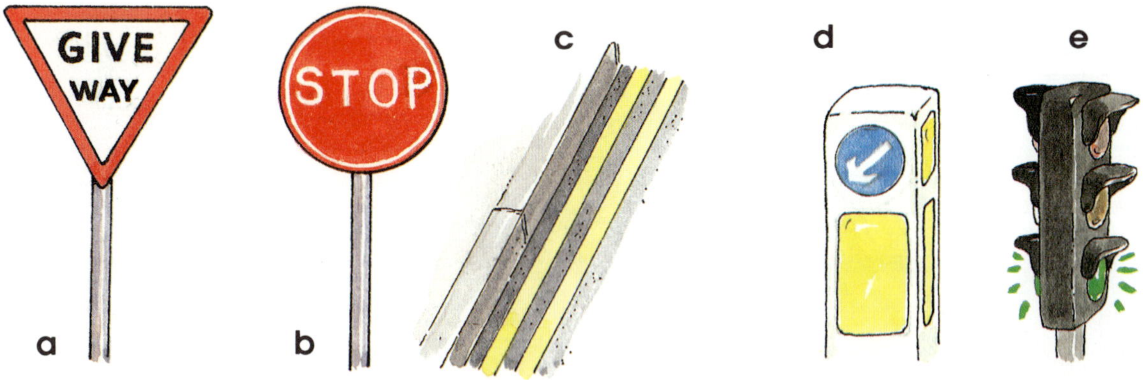

4. These signs show rules for the road. Find out what they mean. Why are they needed?

Sign	Meaning	Why needed
a		
b		

5. List some rules for another place or situation. What might happen if there were no rules?

6. Some rules are made for everyone who lives in the same country. Find out who makes laws. Why does a country have laws?

What happens if people disobey laws?

What do you think about rules and laws?

The local community

A community is a place where people live together.
This picture shows parts of a community.

1. Think why each of these buildings is useful to people in a community.

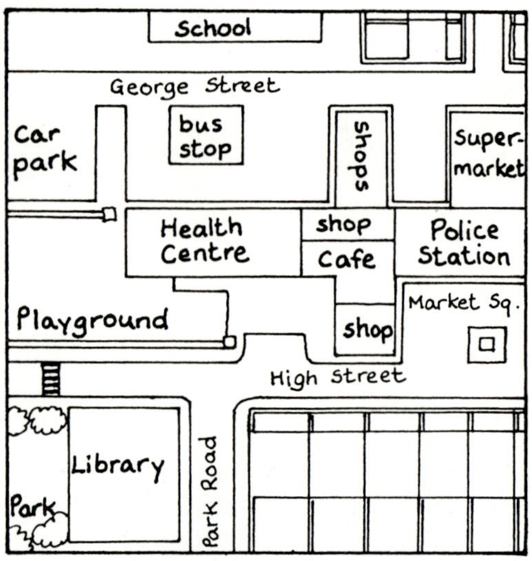

Place	Why it is useful
school	
shops	
library	

2. In a group, find a map of your local area, or draw one. Mark the useful buildings on your map. Design a key.

Some people have jobs that help the community.

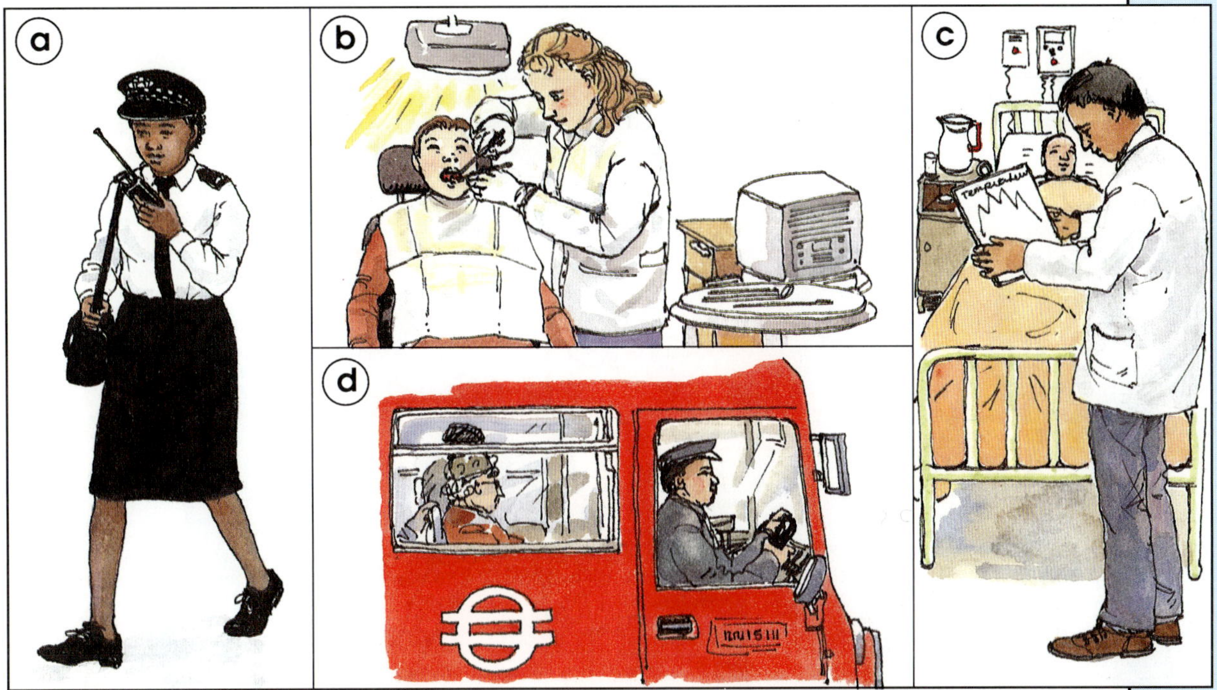

3. How do these people help the community? Copy and complete the chart.
Think of people who help your community and add them to your chart.

Picture	Job	Help for the community
a	police officer	
b		

4. People who live near to each other are neighbours.
Make a list of your neighbours.

5. How can neighbours help each other?

How could you help people in your community?

Conflict

Feelings in quarrels

____________ , ____________ and ____________

are together. ____________ is alone.

1. Draw a picture to show what happened before the scene shown in the picture.

Compare pictures with a friend.

2. Draw a picture to show what you think happened afterwards.

   Write the story.

   How did the children in your story feel?

Children	How they felt
Sam	
Jodie	
Chris	

3. Why do friends quarrel? List five ways to stay friends after a quarrel.

I quarrelled with Jodie about what we would play. We could take turns to choose.

4. In a group, list ways that the people in this story could make it a happy ending

5. Copy and complete these sentences:

I find it easy to say 'sorry' when ______________ .

I find it hard to say 'sorry' when ______________ .

What could you do next time you quarrel with a friend?

Things that influence us

Advertisements

Advertisements often try to persuade people to do things, go places or buy things.

1. What do these advertisements try to persuade people to do? How do they do this?

Advertisement	What it advertises	How it tries to persuade
a		
b		

2. Look for more advertisements in newspapers, magazines and on television. Listen to radio advertisements. Use the chart to describe them.

3. List some things that you or your family have done or bought after seeing or hearing advertisements.

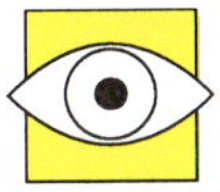
4. What does this advertisement tell you about *Fun Fruiteez*? What does it <u>not</u> tell you?

5. Make an advertisement that tells everything about *Fun Fruiteez*. Make a jingle to go with it.

6. Advertisements are persuaders. Sometimes other people, even friends, try to persuade you to do things. Finish this story:

What can you do if someone tries to persuade you to do something you think is foolish or wrong?

Hygiene

Keeping clean

Health

1. Which of the things in the picture do people need to keep themselves clean?

Things that we really need	Things that are nice to have

Think about parts of the body that need special care.

2. What should people do to keep clean:
   - in the morning?
   - at night?
   - at other times?

3. Why should they do these things?

Here is a day in Lucy's life.
How does she keep her teeth healthy?

4. List the things that Lucy does to keep her teeth healthy.

5. With friends, make up a song about keeping teeth healthy.

Here are some ideas to help:

cleaning	food
toothbrush	dentist
toothpaste	decay
sugar	rot
sweets	bad
filling	fresh

How could you make sure you have healthy habits?

Microbes

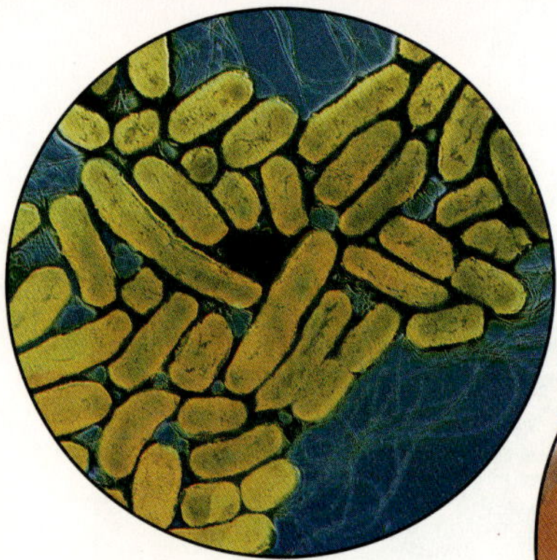

The bacteria that cause salmonella poisoning.

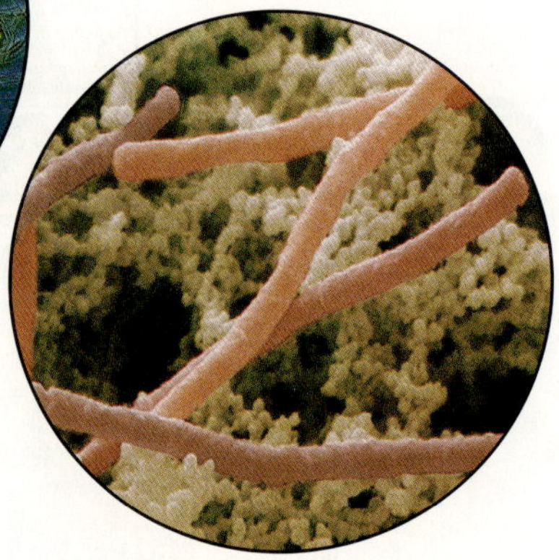

The bacteria in live yoghurt.

Germs are tiny.
We can only see them using a powerful microscope.

The proper name for a germ is a microbe. Bacteria, fungi and viruses are microbes.

Some microbes are useful in making foods. They do not do us any harm.

1. Describe the microbes in the photographs. What do they make you think about?

2. Collect wrappers and pictures of foods that contain bacteria or fungi. Make a classroom display with your labels and wrappers.

3. Copy and complete this chart about helpful microbes.

Microbe	Food	What the microbe does
yeast	bread	makes it rise

4. Use a dictionary to find out what 'contaminated' and 'infected' mean.

Some illnesses are caused by microbes getting into our bodies.

Microbes can get into the body in different ways: through the air, from contaminated food or water, if infected blood gets into your body.

5. Look at the pictures and decide how microbes cause illness in each picture. What should the children in each picture have done?

Picture	How the germs spread	What the children should have done
a		
b		

6. Find out about white blood cells, which fight microbes in our bodies.

How can you make sure you do not have any infections?

Food

How food helps us

Foods that build healthy bones, muscles, skin and blood.

Foods that give energy.

Food that help our bodies to get rid of waste.

Foods that give our bodies the water they need.

1. Use the pictures to plan three healthy meals that you would enjoy eating.
This chart may help:

Meal	For healthy bones, muscles, skin and blood	For energy	To keep our bodies working properly	For water

2. Draw what you ate yesterday. Tick the foods that gave you energy.

You could draw the foods that make the meals healthy.

Most food comes from animals or plants.
What foods come from these animals and plants?

a

b

e

f

c

d

g

h

3. Make animal and plant food charts:

Animal	Foods
a	
b	

Plant	Foods
e	
f	

Often our food comes in packets, jars or tins.

4. Collect food labels from packets, jars and tins.
Read what is in them.
List any surprises you find.

5. Make pictures to show healthy food for:
- a baby
- you
- someone old.

Look for sugar in foods that are not sweet!

How could you try to make your diet healthier?

What is disability?

Different abilities

We all have different abilities.

1. Discuss with a partner what the children above are doing.

2. Think about what you can and cannot do.

3. Copy and complete the chart.

Things I do well	Things I find difficult	Things I cannot do

People with disabilities have difficulty doing some activities and cannot do others.

Often they can do things that others do not expect.

4. Talk to a partner about the photographs. What do they show about people with disabilities?

5. Most people need help from others at times. What do you need help with?

... reaching high places?

... spelling?

... adding large numbers?

... making hot drinks?

6. Sometimes people want to do things for themselves.
Describe to a partner a time when you felt like this.
Why did you feel this way?
What did you do or say?
What happened?

What sort of help do they not want?

7. Find out what help is needed by people you know.

How can you make sure that what you do to help someone is what they want?

Exercise

Our bodies are like machines

How is your body like a machine?

1. Copy and complete this chart.

What it does or needs	**My body** (✓ ✗)	**Machines** (✓ ✗)
moves		
gets warm		

Exercise is one way to look after your body.
Exercise helps your body to have:

stamina

strength

suppleness

2. Find out what these three words mean.

3. Look at the photographs.
How do the activities help keep the people healthy and fit?

Do they give strength, stamina or suppleness?

Exercise	Strength	Stamina	Suppleness

4. Draw an outline of your body, like this but bigger.
Put a cross on your outline wherever you have a joint.

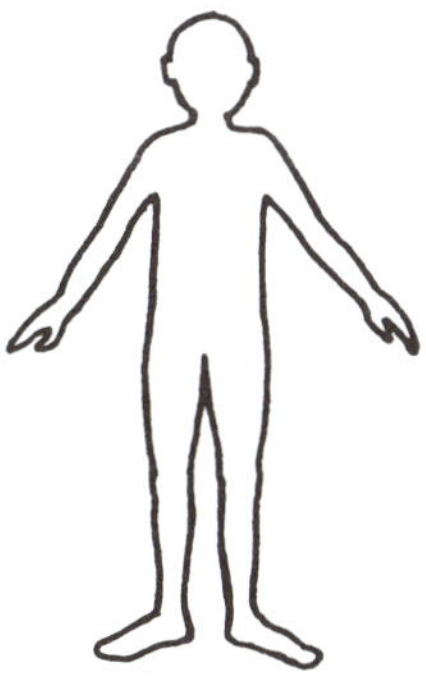

You can bend where there is a joint.

5. Think of some bendy movements to keep your joints supple. Draw and write the instructions for a dance that uses these movements.

6. Draw a poster showing six activities that you would enjoy.

Include some for
- suppleness
- strength
- stamina.

a

b

c

d

Think of some more exercises.

How could you keep yourself healthy and active?

Leisure

How we spend our time

This is how John's family spent their time one Wednesday.

John's mother's day

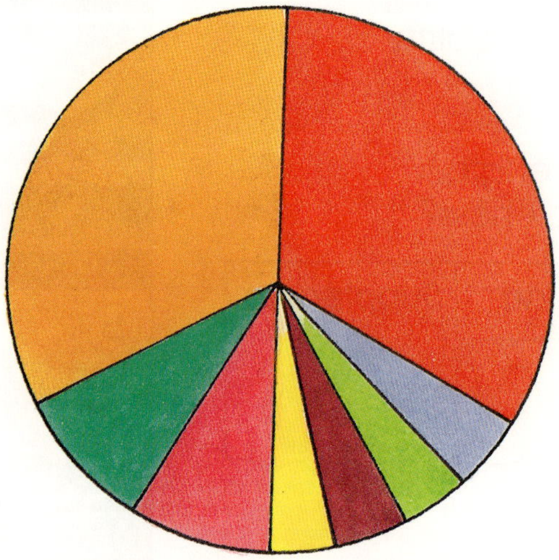

John

7 hours at school
10 hours asleep
$\frac{1}{2}$ hour walking to school
$\frac{1}{2}$ hour homework
$\frac{1}{2}$ hour washing and dressing
$\frac{1}{2}$ hour tidying up and washing up
2 hours computer games
1 hour football
2 hours watching TV

John's mother

8 hours at work
8 hours asleep
1 hour washing and dressing
1 hour travelling by car
1 hour watching TV
1 hour reading
2 hours cooking, cleaning and eating
2 hours with family

John's father

8 hours at work
8 hours asleep
1 hour washing and dressing
1 hour travelling by train
1 hour cooking, cleaning and eating
1 hour with family
1 hour gardening
2 hours watching TV
1 hour reading

1. Look at John's mother's pie chart. How did she spend most of her time?

2. Make pie charts for John and his father. Use different colours to show what they did.

3. How much time did each person spend at work and leisure?

	John	Father
work		
leisure		

4. Make a pie chart to show how you spent one day.

What is the difference between work and leisure?

5. Copy and complete the chart.

Activity	Work or leisure?
digging	
writing	

Add some activities of your own to the chart.

6. What are your three favourite ways of enjoying yourself?

7. Make a tally chart and a graph to show what children in your class do for leisure.

What is the most popular activity?

Which pastimes are energetic? Which are relaxed?

8. Make a list to show how you spent your time yesterday.

What energetic things did you do? What relaxed things did you do?

Class 4 leisure	
reading	卌 卌 I 卌 卌
swimming	卌 卌 卌
football	卌 卌 II

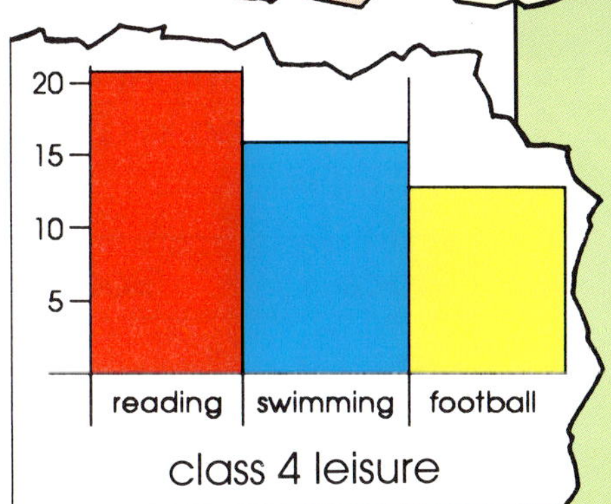

How could you plan to use your leisure time?

Our environment

Looking around

Our environment is where we live.

1. Which of these places is most like where you live?

2. Talk to a partner about the pictures and about where you live.

What is good about the place you live?

What might be good about the other places?

3. What might not be so good about each place? Working in a group, list as many things as you can.

Place	Good points	Bad points
a		

4. Draw and describe a place where you would like to live. What is good about it? These ideas may help.

It is very quiet and pretty.
It might be lonely.
There are lots of trees.
The shops are far away.

5. Sometimes people spoil the place they live in. In a group, talk about how these places have been spoiled.

6. List things that spoil where you live.

Things that spoil the place	How they spoil it

Word bank

vandalism	pollution
graffiti	rubbish
dumping	fumes

7. Choose one of the things on your list. Make a poster persuading people not to do it.

What could you do to look after your environment?

Change

My growing self

1. Which one of these pictures shows someone about the same age as you?

2. You used to be like some of the others. What were you like when you were younger?

Make a chart.

Age	What I looked like	What I could do	What I could not do
When I was born			
1			
3			
5			

3. Continue the chart to show what you are like now.

4. Think about important things that have happened to you.
Make a time line to show them.

This is Gwenan's time line.

I was born.	I went into hospital.	My baby sister was born.	I went to playgroup.	I started school.	I went to Disneyland.

5. What was better about being younger?
What is better about being your age?

6. Talk to your group about who looked after you when you were younger. What did they do for you?

7. Think about something or someone that you look after. What do you do for them?

8. Draw and write some instructions for looking after something or somebody.

What do you like about being your age?

My growing body

Changes and growth

These people are all different ages.

a

b

c

d

e

f

1. Which people are older than you?
How can you tell they are older?
How are they different from you?

	Same or older?	How can you tell?
a		
b		

2. You have grown and changed a lot since you were born.
You will change and grow some more until you are grown up.

How will you change between now and:
- age 12
- age 17?

3. How has the person in these photographs changed?

My Grandad when he was nine.

My Grandad now. He is taller and fatter. His head is a bit bald. He has a beard and a moustache.

These objects are linked to growing up.

4. How old would someone be when they first use these things?

Explain your answers.

Object	Age	Reason
a		
b		

5. Draw and describe some more things that people use when they are grown up.

What is better about being:
– your age?
– grown up?

What do you look forward to about growing up?

New baby

Reproduction

These women are pregnant.
Soon they will each have a baby.

The inside story

a

b

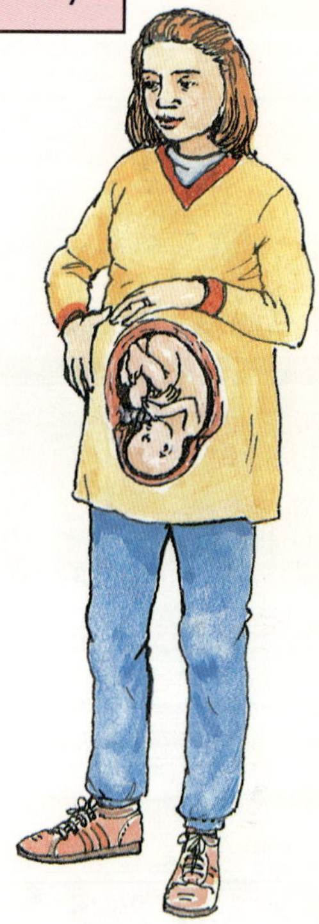

Before it is born, the baby does not need to eat or breathe. It gets all it needs from inside its mother's body. It grows bigger, wriggles and kicks.

1. How can you tell from picture **a** that the women are pregnant?

   How do you think the woman in picture **b** feels?

2. A baby grows from an egg.
   All animals grow from eggs.
   Draw a hen's egg, life size.
   Next to it draw a life-size frog's egg.
   Then draw a butterfly's egg. Finally, draw a human egg, the size of a pinpoint.

3. Find out about other animals' eggs.
   Which ones grow inside their mothers?
   Which hatch outside?

Animal	Eggs grow inside	Hatch outside

Before a woman's egg can grow into a baby it has to be joined by a sperm from a man.

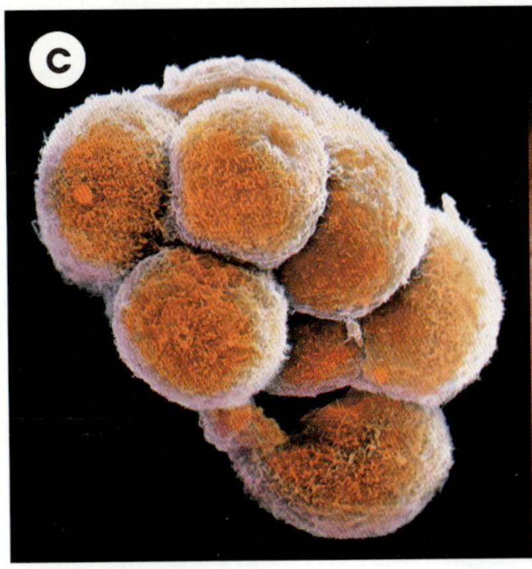

The sperm and egg join together.

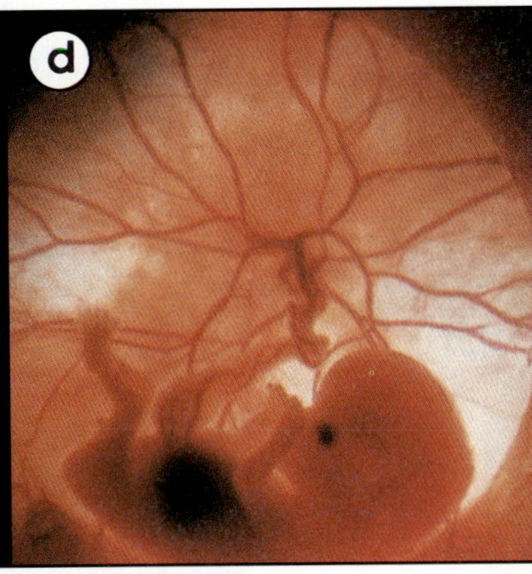

They grow into a baby.

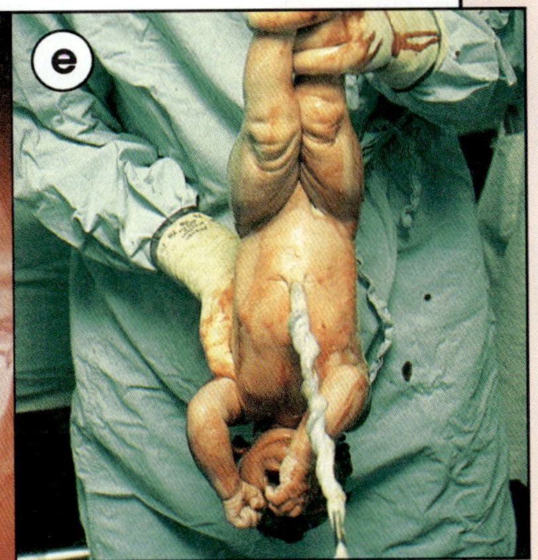

About nine months later the baby is born.

4. What changes can you see, from egg to baby?

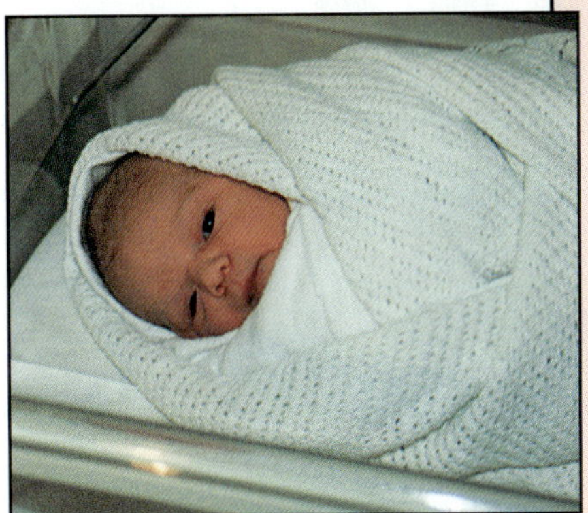

What can a new-born baby do?
What can't it do?
What has to be done for it?

As the baby grows, he or she can do more.

5. Find out when babies learn to do different things, such as walk, talk and feed themselves.

Age	What the baby can do
2 months	Eat solid food.
	Sit up.

6. Collect pictures of things that babies need. Why do they need them? Display what you have discovered.

How do you feel when you see a newborn baby?

Families

Belonging to a family

This is Geeta. She lives with her mother, father, grandmother, Auntie Bhavna and brothers Anhil and Nimish.

There are all kinds of families. Here are some other families.

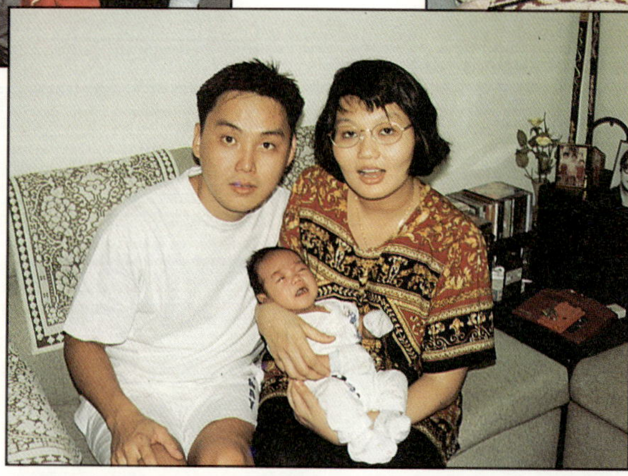

1. In what ways are these families similar to each other? How are they different?

2. Draw your family. Why do you call these people your family?

Family words

mother	auntie	grandmother	step mother
father	uncle	niece	step father
sister	cousin	nephew	adopted child
brother	grandfather	carer	guardian

Families may not all live together in the same house.
These pictures show people from the same family.

3. Describe the family in the pictures.
How can you tell that they are a family?

4. List the people in your family who live with you and those who do not live with you.

My family	
Live with me	Do not live with me

Families have different ways of showing that they care about each other.

5. What do people in your family do to show that they care about each other?

How do you show care for your family?

There are many jobs to do in families.

6. Who does which jobs in your family?
Make a list of all the jobs that are done and who does them.

Job	Who does it?
washing up	
cooking	
cleaning	
shopping	

So ... what will you do to show that you care and to help your family?

Secrets

Good and bad secrets

Secrets can be fun.

1. What was the secret in the story? Describe any secrets like this that you have kept.

2. Picture **a** shows a different kind of secret. How is it different?

3. Write a story to describe what is happening in picture **a**. Describe how all the children feel.

4. Complete these sentences.

An example of a good secret ______________________________

An example of a bad secret ______________________________

Sometimes people ask us to keep secrets that we think we should not keep or that make us feel unhappy.

5. What should you do about these secrets? Discuss it with a partner. Record your ideas.

Unhappy secrets

What we should do.

6. Finish the poem *Can you keep a secret?* You could make it rhyme. Re-draft and illustrate your poem.

Telling someone else can help us feel better about unwanted secrets. Who could these children tell?

7. What should the children in the pictures do? Should they tell? Why?

b The children should ______ because ____________.

c The girl and boy watching should ______ because ____________.

d The girl should ______ because ____________.

If you are asked to keep a secret, what will you think about?

Feeling safe

Being in charge

Sometimes people we know and feel safe with ask us to do things that we do not want to do.

Rachel has to go to Auntie June's house every day. But she wants to play with her friends.

One day she told her dad that she did not want to go to Auntie June's house.

Rachel's dad took Auntie June out to meet people. Family, friends and neighbours began to visit her.

1. Draw the next picture for this story. Add speech bubbles and thought bubbles to the picture.

2. What do people ask children to do? Talk to a partner about what children should or should not do.

Copy and complete the chart.

Things children are asked to do	Should they do this?

Explain your answers.
How can another trusted adult help?

Key Idea: Safe people

You are in charge of your body.
Sometimes it feels good to be touched.
Sometimes people touch you in a way
or in a place that you do not like.

Ahmed does not like being tickled.

Pete does not like his big brother wrestling with him.

Ann does not like her Mum's boyfriend to cuddle her.

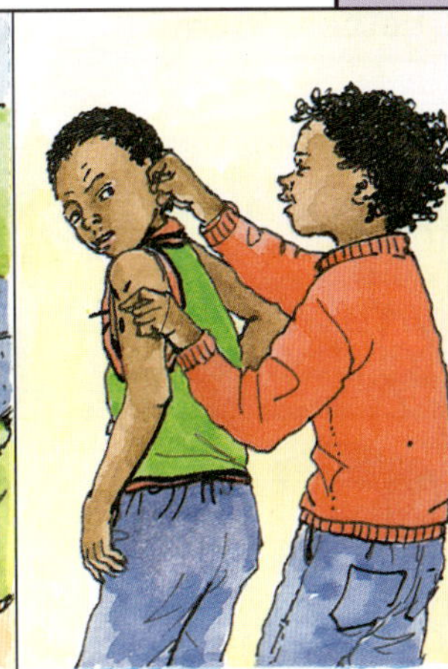

Nick does not like his cousin pinching him.

3. How did each child feel?
What could they do?

4. Sometimes we do not feel safe when strangers talk to us.

Draw a stranger. Compare it with a friend's drawing.

5. Sometimes it is safe to talk to strangers.
When?
Make a poster to show strangers you can talk to.

If you feel unsafe, what will you do?

Harmful materials

Drugs

Drugs change how our mind and body work. When we are ill drugs (medicines) can help. Which pictures show when drugs are safe?

1. Copy and complete the chart.

Picture	Safe or unsafe
a	
b	

Some medicines stop us becoming ill. Some help our body fight illness. Some stop us feeling pain. Some help us cope with illness.

Medicine	What it is for
aspirin	headache
insulin	diabetes

2. In a group, think of an example of each kind of medicine.
Who might need them?

3. What medicines do you know? With a partner, draw and list them and show what they are for.

Only take medicine from a trusted adult.

Key Idea: Helpful and harmful drugs

Some people take drugs when they are not ill.
They use the drug to alter their state of mind or how they feel.
This can harm their bodies and their minds.

4. What drugs do you know about that people use? How do they use them?

How people use it				
drug	smoke	sniff	swallow	inject
nicotine (cigarettes)				

You may know people who use alcohol and cigarettes as drugs.

5. Describe how alcohol might affect the people in the picture. What foolish decisions have the people made? What sensible decision have they made?

Cigarettes can also harm people.
Most people know about the harm but some people still choose to smoke.

6. Carry out a survey to find out:
a) why people started smoking
b) why they don't stop.

7. Make up an advertising jingle to persuade people not to smoke or drink alcohol.

What could you do if you are offered harmful drugs?

Dangerous places

Spotting dangers

Homes can be dangerous.

1. List the dangers in these pictures.

Dangers	
Picture a	Picture b

2. Draw another part of the house in the picture, such as a living room, hall or bathroom. Include some dangers in your drawing.
   Ask a partner to list the dangers in your picture.
   Re-draw one of the pictures but this time make it safe.
   Label what you have changed.

3. Collect pictures of things that can harm you at home.
   Explain how they can be kept safe.

Signs in the environment help us to keep safe.
How do these signs help us?

4. Copy and complete the chart.

Sign	What it tells us	How it keeps us safe
a		
b		

5. Draw any safety signs that you have seen at home, at school or out and about.

Signs tell us things by their shape and colour.

6. Match the instructions to these road sign outlines.

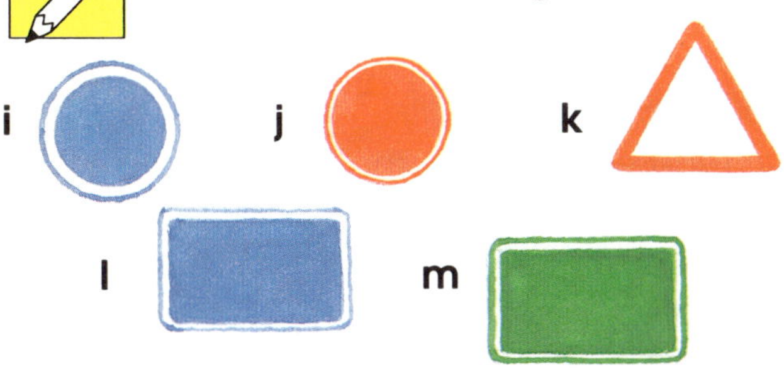

Meaning	Sign
Do something	
Do not do something	
Information	
Warning	
Instruction	

7. Design some signs to use in your school.

What can you do to make sure you are safe at home, school and out and about?

Glossary

Here are some words used in this book that may be new to you. The number in brackets shows the page where the word is first used.

ability (24) What somebody can do.

alcohol (45) A drink that can make people drunk. A kind of drug.

asthma (44) A disease that can make breathing difficult.

auntie (38) Father or mother's sister.

bacteria (20) Tiny living things. Some bacteria can cause disease. Some are useful. (The singular is bacterium.)

cell (21) A very small part of any living thing. Cells can only be seen using a powerful microscope. White blood cells fight infections.

community (12) A group of people who live in a close area or work together.

conflict (14) A disagreement.

consequences (5) The results of actions.

cousin (38) The child of an **aunt** or **uncle**.

disability (24) A condition that stops people doing some things.

drug (44) A material used as a **medicine**, to cure or prevent illness or as a painkiller. A material that some people use to alter their state of mind.

features (2) Parts of the face: for example, the nose, mouth or eyes.

fungi (20) A plant-like living thing that lives and feeds on plants or animals. (The singular is fungus.)

hygiene (18) Cleanliness (being clean).

leisure (28) Free time to do what you please.

medicine (44) A **drug** that is used to prevent or cure illness or as a painkiller.

microbe (20) A tiny living thing that can only be seen using a powerful microscope. **Bacteria** and **viruses** are microbes.

nephew (38) Son of an **auntie** or **uncle**.

niece (38) Daughter of an **auntie** or **uncle**.

pregnant (36) Having a baby developing inside the body.

qualities (6) Things that are special about a person.

sperm (37) A cell from a man that can fertilise an egg so that it will grow into a baby. A cell from any male animal that can fertilise an egg from a female animal of the same kind.

stamina (26) The ability to keep going in a physical activity, such as running or swimming.

strength (26) Being strong.

suppleness (26) Being able to bend and stretch the body.

uncle (38) Father or mother's brother.

virus (20) Tiny living thing that lives only in the cells of an animal or plant. Many viruses cause diseases.

Usborne

That's not my...
Christmas
Activity book

Rosie Dickins

Illustrated by Rachel Wells

Designed by
Josephine Thompson & Hannah Ahmed

Based on the best-selling *That's not my...* touchy-feely series

That's my elf

Trace the dotted letters if you like.

Can you find the little white mouse?

Fill in your elf's hat and buttons.

Which present has a BLUE ribbon?

Can you GIGGLE like an elf?

That's my robin

Fill in the rest of your robin.

Where is the little white mouse?

Can you CHIRP like a robin?

Can you find two robins that MATCH?

That's my snowman

Finish your snowman's hat, scarf and mittens.

Spot the little white mouse.

Count my buttons... 1... 2... 3.
Where do these footprints lead?
Find two carrot noses.

That's my tree

Can you see the little white mouse?

Fill in the stars.

Can you show the car
the way to drive home?

Find a reindeer
in the snow.

Where is the
little white
mouse hiding?

Fill in your
decoration.

That's my decoration

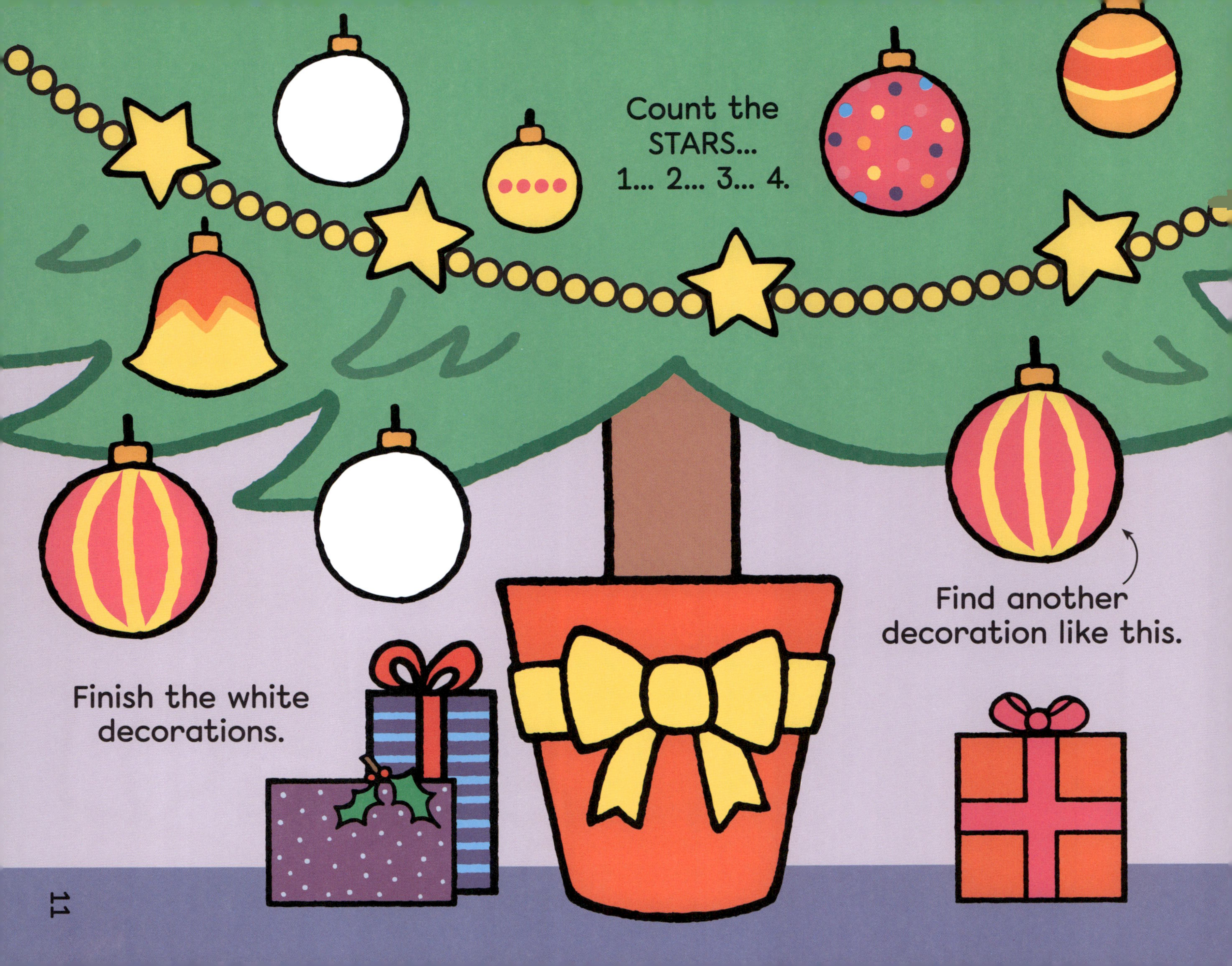
Count the
STARS...
1... 2... 3... 4.
Find another
decoration like this.
Finish the white
decorations.

That's my reindeer

Decorate your reindeer's harness.

Little white mouse, where are you?

One reindeer has a GREEN harness. Can you find it?
Which of us has a WHITE tummy?
Find a reindeer with SPOTS.

That's my angel

Finish your angel's dress and hair.

Find the little white mouse.

Can you find two decorations that MATCH?

Fill in this angel's dress.

That's my snowflake

Join the dots to finish your snowflake.

Little white mouse, are you there?

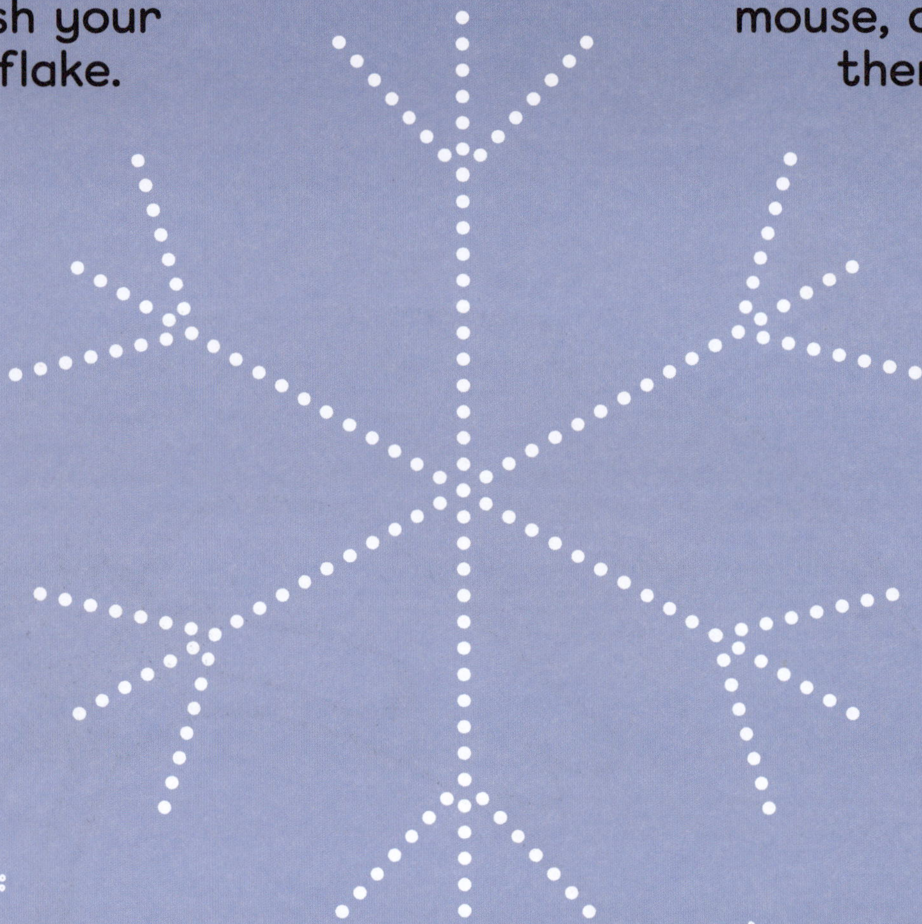

Count the YELLOW stars...
1... 2... 3... 4... 5.

Find two BLUE snowflakes.

Can you say HELLO to Santa?

That's my fairy

Can you see the little white mouse?

Spot the differences between these pictures.
There are THREE to find.

Where is the little white mouse now?

Fill in your stocking.

That's my stocking

Which little stocking is the odd one out?

Find a PINK present.

That's my sleigh

Can you spot
the little
white mouse?

Uh-oh, FIVE presents have fallen in the snow. Can you find them all?

Who is packing the sleigh?

Can you spot a GREEN present?

Who has a RED scarf?

That's my present

Find the little white mouse.

Finish the pattern on your present.

Follow the trails to see
who gets which present.

Who is
getting a
MAGICAL
present?

That's my Santa

Finish Santa's hat.

Can you say HO-HO-HO like Santa Claus?

Can you see the little white mouse?

Now Santa is climbing down a chimney. Fill in his boots.
Can you find a house with TWO chimneys?
Who is walking in the snow?

That's my Christmas

Where is the little white mouse NOW?

Can you spot the differences between these scenes?
There are FIVE to find.

Who has woken up?

Can you name these Christmas things?

Present

Angel

Sleigh

Robin

Santa

Snowflake

Reindeer

Can you see
3 mice with
SCARVES?

Find a mouse
with a PRESENT.

Can you
SQUEAK like
a mouse?

Who is NOT
a mouse?

Stocking

Fairy

Tree

Decoration

Mouse

Elf

Snowman